Contents

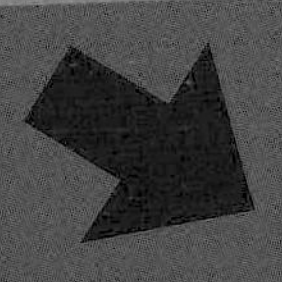

Some words are shown in bold, **like this.** You can find out what they mean by looking in the glossary.

Why Make Healthy Choices?

Just as computers run on electricity, your body runs on food and water. You need food and water in order to think, move, and grow. Healthy foods contain more **nutrients** for your body than unhealthy foods. If you make healthy choices, you will feel and look your best.

Try to drink at least six glasses of plain water every day.

To work properly, your body needs different kinds of foods in the right amounts for your age and size. People who eat healthy foods have lots of energy. They are sick less often than those who eat unhealthy foods.

What Makes a Lunch Healthy or Unhealthy?

It is important to eat lunch to keep up your energy levels in the middle of the day. Some lunch foods are much less healthy than others. For instance, French fries are usually high in **saturated fat**, which can clog up your heart and blood vessels.

Chicken noodle soup from a can is often high in **sodium**, which is bad for your heart.

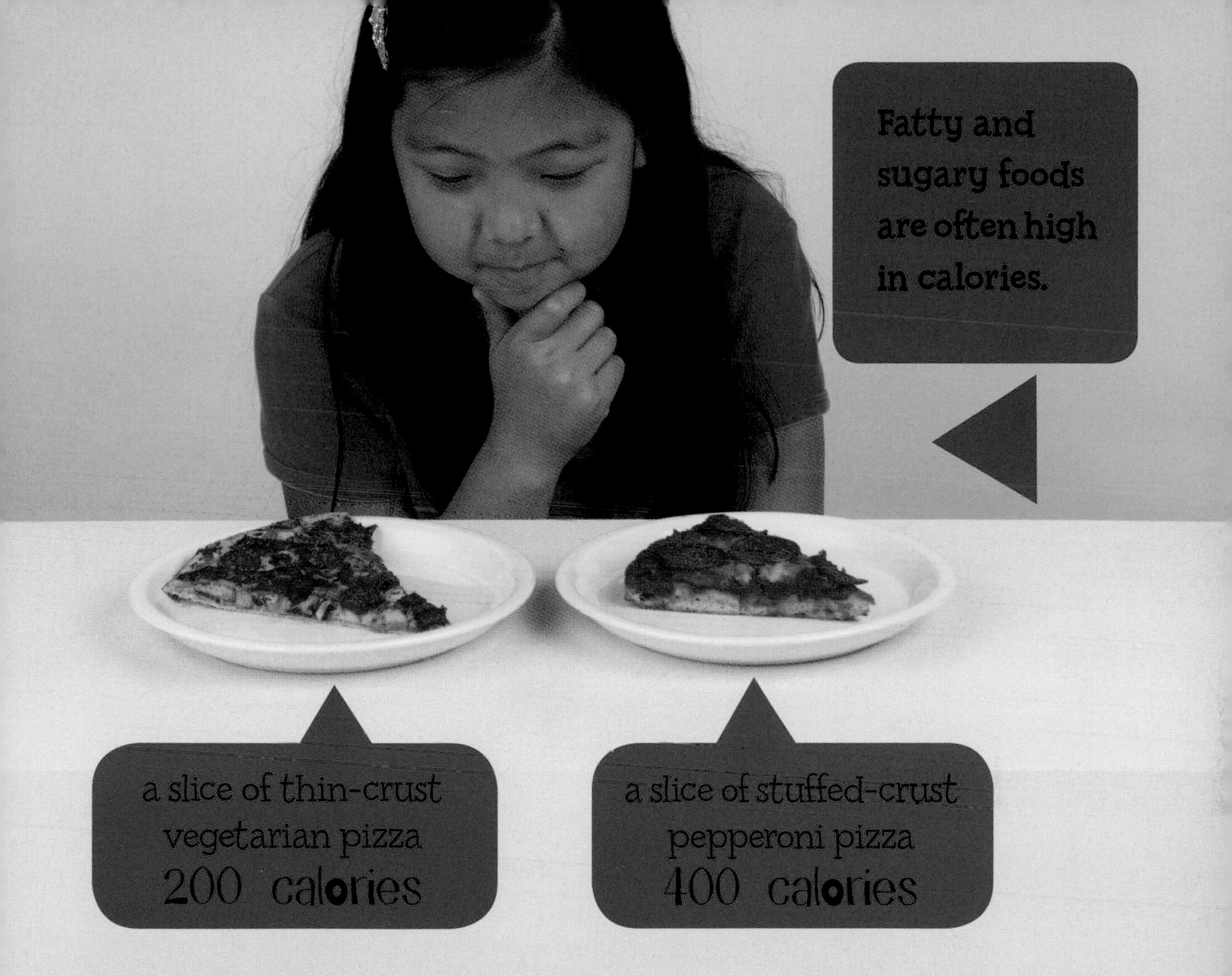

The energy food gives you is measured in **calories.** You need a certain amount of calories per day to stay healthy, depending on your age, your height, and how much exercise you get. Eating too many or too few calories every day can make you **overweight** or too thin.

Savory Sandwiches

A sandwich may look healthy, but it can be packed with unhealthy ingredients. White bread lacks **fiber**, which keeps your stomach working. It is low in **vitamins** and **minerals**, which your body needs to grow and to repair itself. Fillings made from **processed** foods can be high in **saturated fat** and **sodium.**

A sandwich can contain more fat and calories than some people should eat in a day.

Whole grain bread contains lots of fiber, vitamins, and minerals. Also, the energy you get from it lasts longer than energy from white bread. Low-fat dressings and fillings of fresh vegetables and **lean** fresh meats give your body **nutrients** without saturated fat or too many **calories**.

Sweet Sandwiches

Sandwiches with sweet fillings, such as jam, honey, or chocolate hazelnut spread, can be tasty for lunch, but they are full of sugar, which your body uses up quickly. This can mean your energy level suddenly drops in the afternoon.

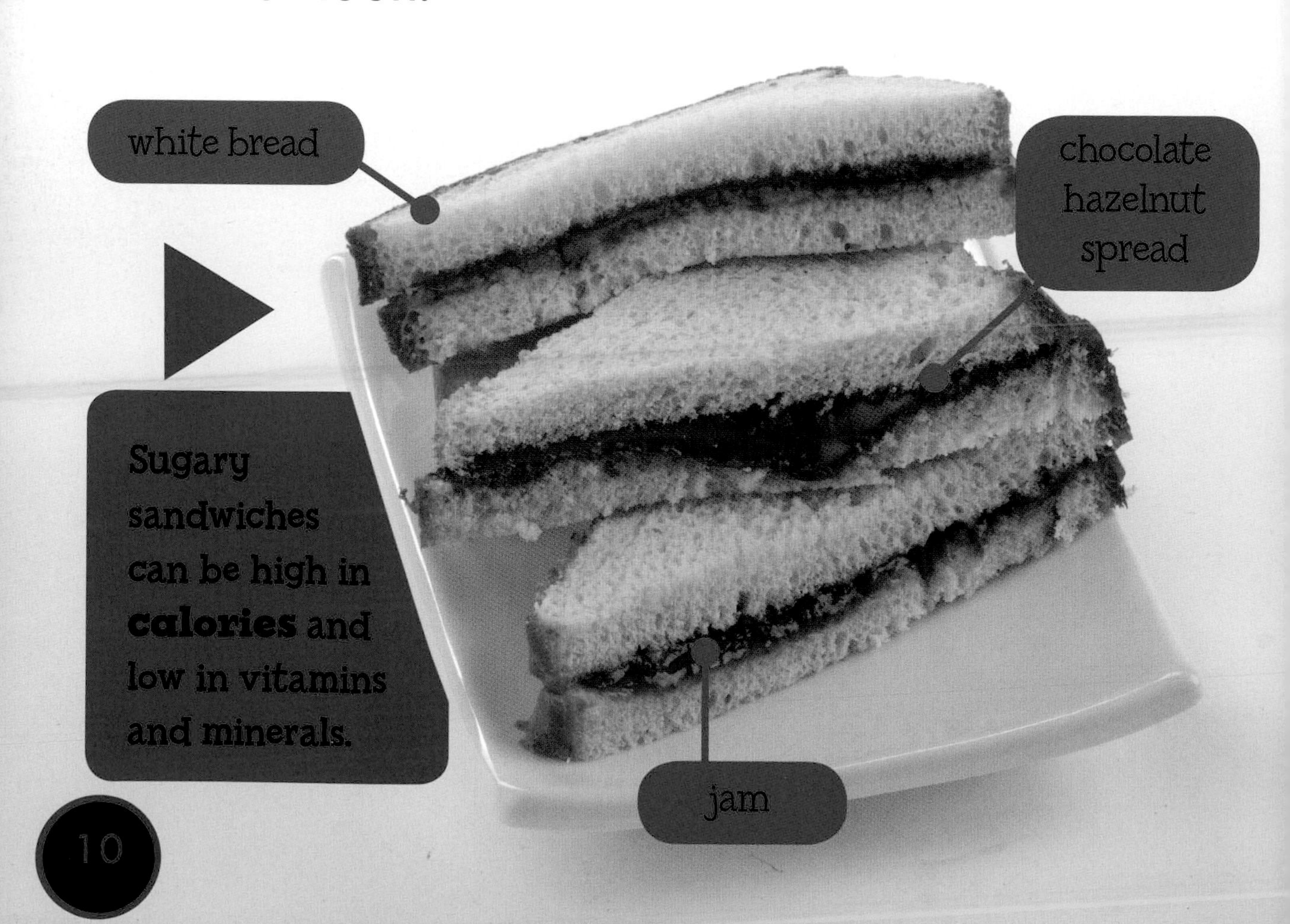

Sugary sandwiches can be high in **calories** and low in vitamins and minerals.

You can use **whole grain** bread instead of white bread for energy that lasts longer. There are also sweet fillings you can choose that have both long-lasting energy and lots of **fiber, vitamins**, and **minerals.**

Burgers

If you are in a hurry at lunchtime, you may be tempted to choose a hamburger and fries from a fast-food restaurant. These are usually high in **saturated fat, sodium,** and **calories.**

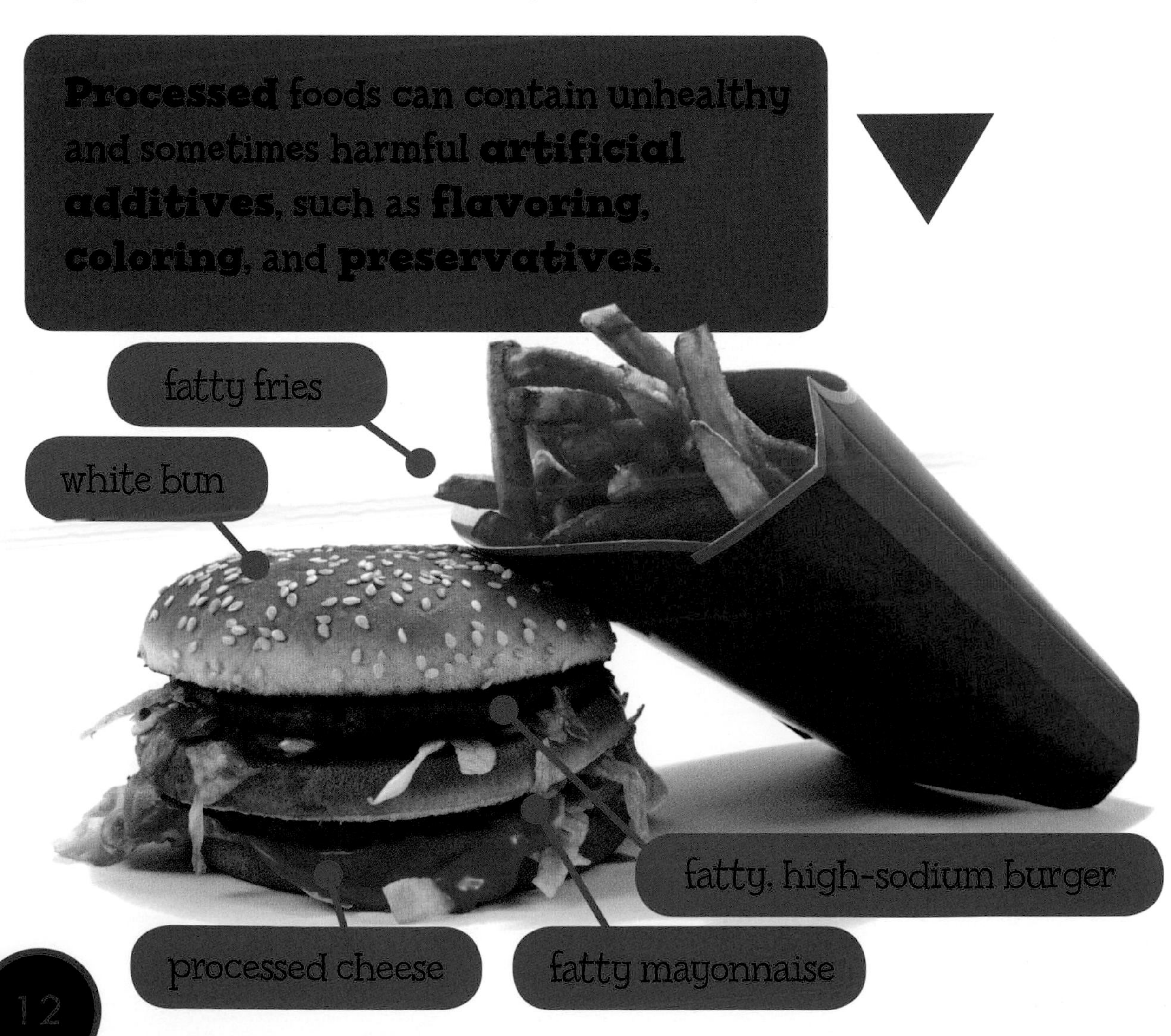

Processed foods can contain unhealthy and sometimes harmful **artificial additives**, such as **flavoring**, **coloring**, and **preservatives.**

A burger freshly made from turkey is healthier. Turkey is **leaner** than beef, so it has less saturated fat. It is still rich in **protein,** which your body needs to build skin and muscle. Choose a **whole grain** bun for **fiber,** with low-fat mayonnaise, and carrot sticks instead of fries, for **vitamins** and **minerals.**

A grilled burger has much less saturated fat than a fried burger.

Hot Dogs

Meat sausages such as hot dogs give our bodies **protein.** However, they are a **processed** food that can be full of **artificial additives** such as **preservatives, coloring,** and **flavoring.** They are also usually high in **saturated fat** and **sodium.**

Hot dogs are a tasty treat, but not healthy as an everyday lunch.

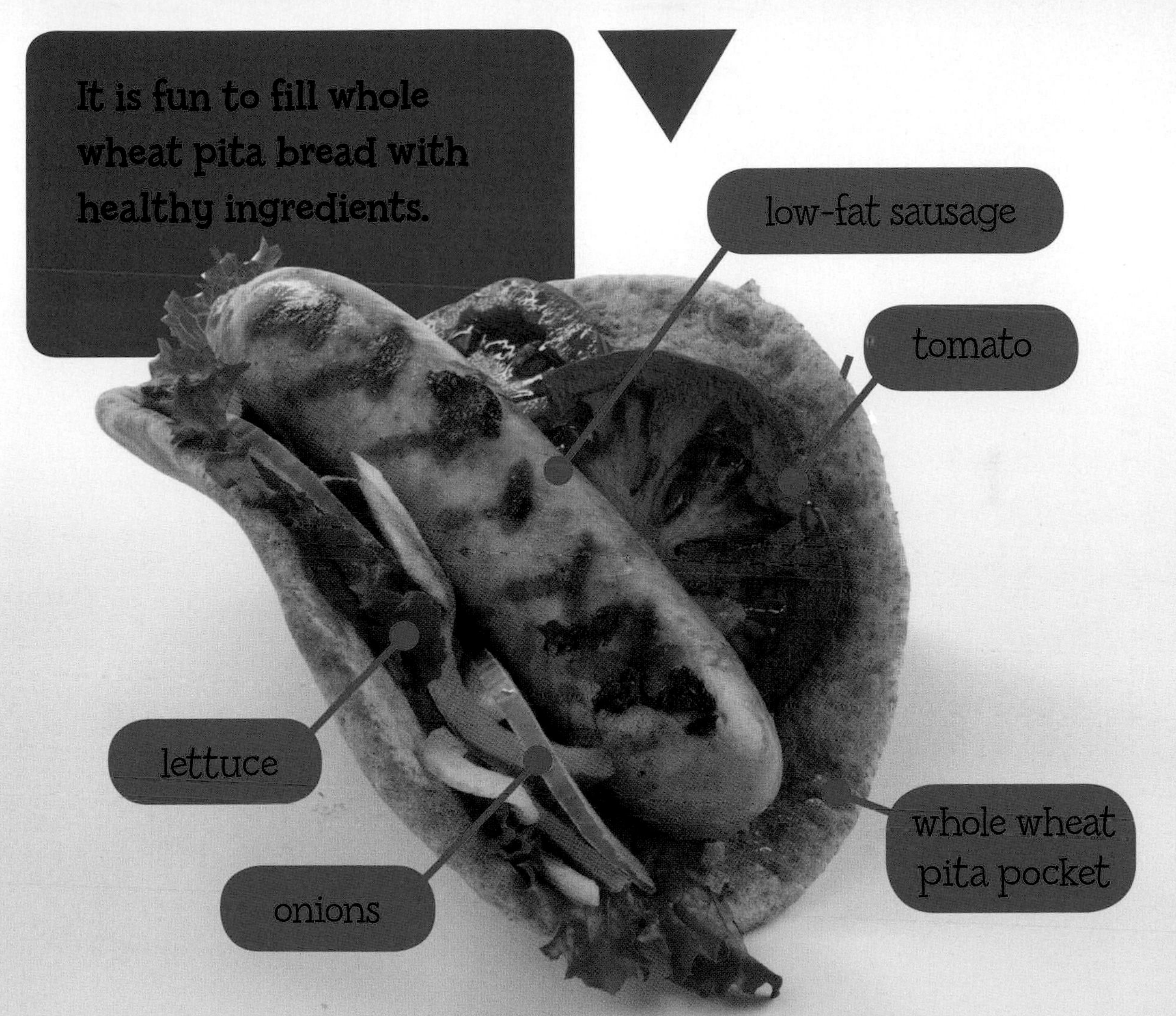

It is fun to fill whole wheat pita bread with healthy ingredients.

Low-fat sausages are a much healthier option. They are still high in protein, but much lower in unhealthy saturated fat. Eat them in **whole wheat** pita bread for longer-lasting energy and lots of **fiber**. Add lettuce and vegetables for plenty of **vitamins** and **minerals**.

Chicken

Chicken is a fantastic low-fat source of **protein**. However, coating it and frying it as nuggets makes it high in **saturated fat** and **calories**—especially when eaten with added French fries and coleslaw made with full-fat mayonnaise.

Fried chicken may be delicious, but it is unhealthy to eat it often.

Make your own healthier nuggets or strips by coating chicken in a mixture of **whole grain** flour, cornflakes, spices, and a little vegetable oil. Oven-baking them won't add fat. Potato wedges baked with their skin on are low in fat and high in **fiber**. Make your own coleslaw from low-fat mayonnaise, too.

Ask an adult to help you make your own healthy chicken strip lunch.

Noodles and Pasta

Just adding boiling water to dried noodles can make a speedy lunch. They give you **carbohydrates** for energy. However, they are a **processed** food that is high in **saturated fat** and **sodium**, and low in **vitamins, minerals,** and **fiber**. They also contain unhealthy **artificial additives.**

Instant noodles don't have many **nutrients** for your body.

A grown-up can prepare pasta for you almost as quickly as instant noodles.

Whole wheat pasta with fresh vegetables is a healthier choice. Whole wheat pasta gives you long-lasting energy, but it is low in fat and sodium. Fresh vegetables steamed or fried in a little vegetable oil are packed with fiber, vitamins, and minerals. Stir in a little tuna for added **protein**.

Soup

Soup can be a warming lunch on a cold day. However, canned soup is often high in **sodium** and **artificial additives.** Even some homemade soups, such as creamy clam chowder, can be high in **saturated fat.**

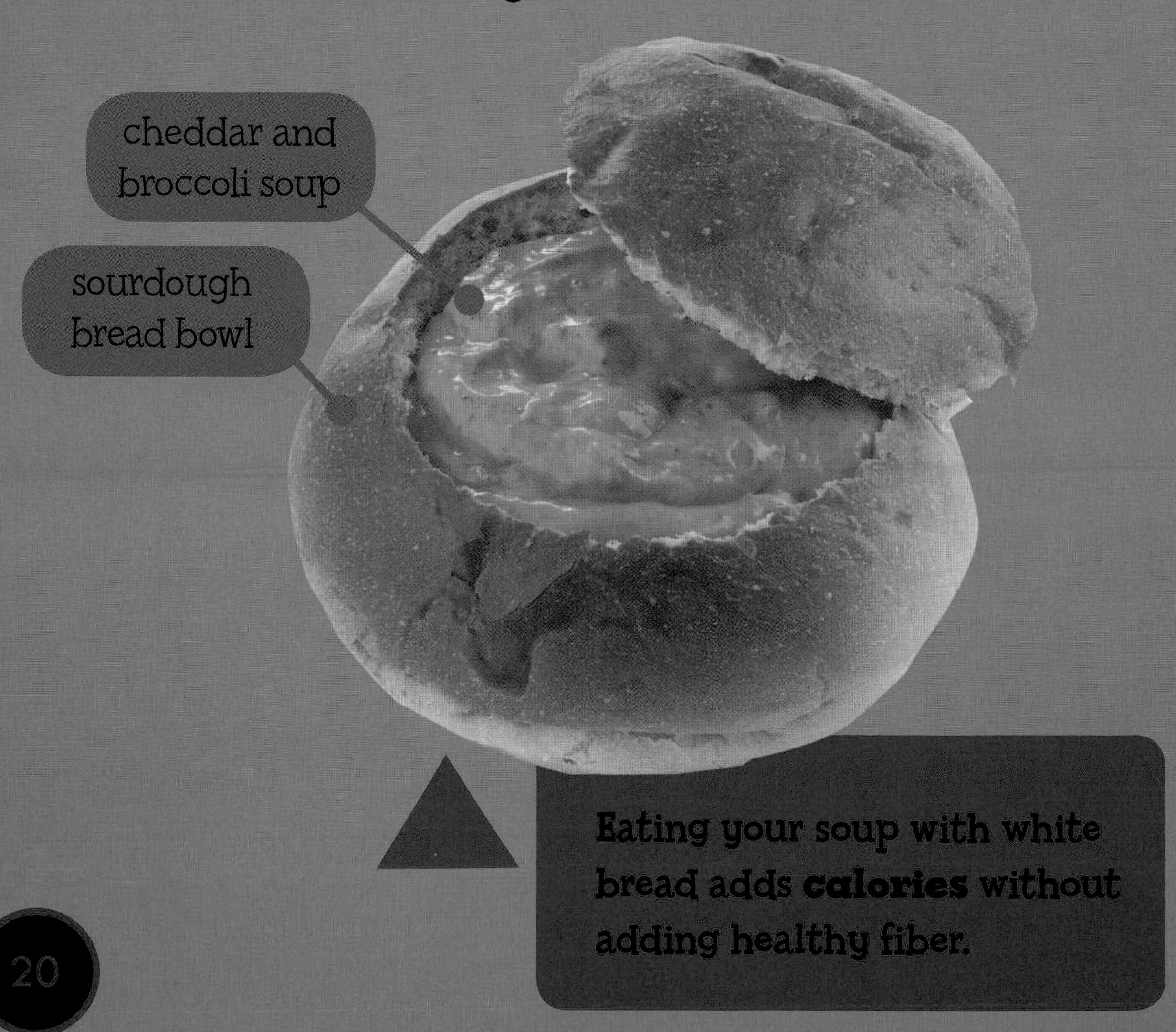

Eating your soup with white bread adds **calories** without adding healthy fiber.

A freshly homemade vegetable soup is usually low in fat and sodium, but it is high in **vitamins**, **minerals**, and healthy **fiber.** If it contains beans, it will be an excellent source of **protein**, too.

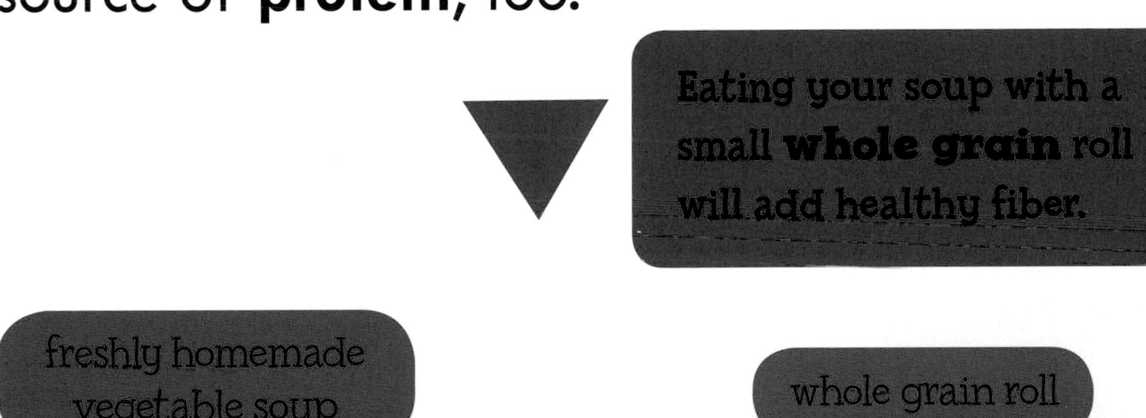
Eating your soup with a small **whole grain** roll will add healthy fiber.

Salads

A salad can be a very healthy choice. However, there are many ingredients that can make salads unhealthy. Store-bought croutons are high in **saturated fat** and **artificial additives.** Cheese can be high in saturated fat and **sodium.** Creamy dressings such as mayonnaise are high in fat and **calories**, too.

Caesar salad is high in fat and calories.

To keep your salads healthy, include grilled white meat or fish for a low-fat source of **protein**. Use plenty of raw vegetables, fruits, nuts, and seeds for **fiber**, **vitamins**, **minerals**, and energy. Leave out fatty **red meats**, croutons, cheese, and creamy or very oily dressings.

You can make a healthy salad dressing by mixing balsamic vinegar and olive oil.

Drinks

Many people like soda with their lunch. A can of soda may contain around 10 teaspoons of sugar, making it very high in **calories**. Soda is often also packed with unhealthy additives such as **caffeine.** Diet drinks are just as unhealthy, since they contain lots of **artificial sweetener**, which can be harmful in large quantities.

Drinking lots of soda can give you **tooth decay**.

A small glass of freshly squeezed fruit juice can be a refreshing drink with your lunch. It is packed with **vitamins** and **minerals.** Avoid many store-bought juices. They are often full of sugar and **artificial additives.** Water is the healthiest drink of all.

Food Quiz

Take a look at these packed lunches. Can you figure out which picture shows an unhealthy lunch and which shows a healthier lunch, and why?

The answer is on the next page.

Food Quiz Answers

This is the unhealthy lunch. The sandwich is high in **saturated fat, sodium,** and **calories.** The chips are also high in saturated fat and sodium, and low in **vitamins** and **minerals.** The chocolate bar and the store-bought fruit juice are both high in sugar.

This is the healthy lunch. The **whole grain** bread sandwich is full of long-lasting energy and **fiber**. The carrot sticks and hummus have lots of vitamins, minerals, and **protein**. The water will help every part of your body work properly. Did you guess correctly?

Tips for Healthy Eating

Use this MyPlate guide to choose the right amounts of different foods for good health. Choose low-fat cooking methods and do not add salt (it is high in **sodium**). Don't forget to drink several glasses of water and to exercise every day.

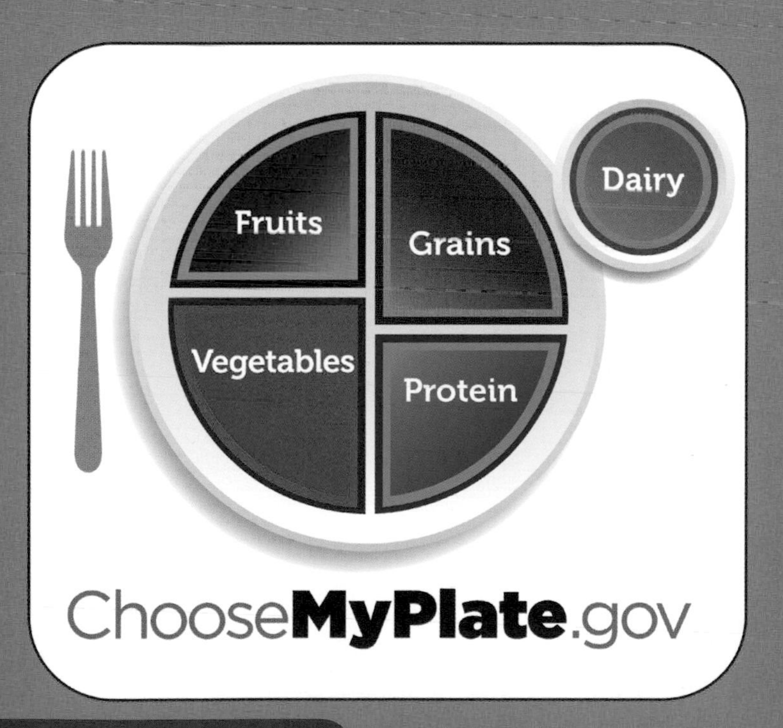

See if you can get the right balance over the course of a whole day.

Glossary

artificial additive human-made substance that is added to food, such as coloring, flavoring, and preservatives

artificial sweetener human-made substance that can be added to food to give it a sweet taste

caffeine substance found in parts of some plants, such as coffee plant seeds and tea bush leaves. When eaten, it makes your brain and nerves work faster than is normal.

calorie unit we use for measuring energy

carbohydrate substance in starchy foods (such as potatoes, pasta, and rice) and sugary foods that gives you energy

coloring something added to food to make it look attractive

fiber part of certain plants that passes through your body without being broken down. This helps other foods to pass through your stomach, too. Some fiber can also help your blood stay healthy.

flavoring something added to food to make it taste better

lean describes meat that has had the fatty parts trimmed off

mineral natural substance, such as iron, that is essential for health

nutrient substance in food that is good for your body, such as vitamins, minerals, and antioxidants

overweight heavier than is healthy for your age and height

preservative something added to food to make it last longer

processed made or prepared in a factory. Processed foods often contain artificial additives.

protein natural substance that your body needs to build skin, muscle, and other tissues. Protein is found in foods such as meat, fish, and beans.

red meat meat, such as beef, lamb, and pork, that is red when raw

saturated fat type of fat found in butter, fatty cuts of meat, cheese, and cream. It is bad for your heart and blood.

sodium natural substance found in salt

tooth decay problem when the outer layers of teeth are dissolved away

vitamin natural substance that is essential for good health

whole grain made with every part of the grain, without removing any of the inner or outer parts

whole wheat made with wheat flour that uses every part of the grain, without removing the inner or outer parts

Find Out More

Books

Graimes, Nicola, and Howard Shooter. *Kids' Fun and Healthy Cookbook*. New York: Dorling Kindersley, 2007.

Parker, Vic. *All About Dairy* (Food Zone). Irvine, Calif.: QEB, 2009.

Veitch, Catherine. *A Balanced Diet* (Healthy Eating with MyPlate). Chicago: Heinemann Library, 2012.

Internet sites

Facthound offers a safe, fun way to find Internet sites related to this book. All of the sites on Facthound have been researched by our staff.

Here's all you do:
Visit **www.facthound.com**
Type in this code: 9781432991173

WWW.FACTHOUND.COM®

Index